C000295082

GEARED FOR GROWTH BIBLE STUDIES

JESUS

-WHO IS HE?

A STUDY IN JOHN'S GOSPEL

BIBLE STUDIES TO IMPACT THE LIVES OF ORDINARY PEOPLE

The Word Worldwide

by John Priddle

CHRISTIAN
FOCUS

ISBN 978-1-84550-699-5

Copyright © WEC International

Published in 2002, reprinted in 2011
by
Christian Focus Publications, Geanies House,
Fearn, Ross-shire, IV20 1TW, Scotland
www.christianfocus.com
and
WEC International, Bulstrode, Oxford Road,
Gerrards Cross, Bucks, SL9 8SZ
www.wecinternational.org

Cover design by Alister MacInnes

Printed and bound by Bell and Bain
Glasgow

Mixed Sources
Product group from well-managed
forests and other controlled sources
www.fsc.org   Cert no. TT-COC-002769
© 1996 Forest Stewardship Council

Contents

PREFACE

**'Where there's LIFE there's GROWTH:
where there's GROWTH there's LIFE.'**

WHY GROW a study group?
Because as we study and share the Bible together, we can:
- learn to combat loneliness, depression, staleness, frustration and other problems,
- get to understand and love one another,
- become responsive to the Holy Spirit's dealing and obedient to God's Word,

and that's **GROWTH.**

HOW do you **GROW** a study group?
- Just start by asking one friend to join you and then aim at expanding your group.
- Study the set portions daily – they are brief and easy: no catches.
- Meet once a week to discuss what you find.
- Befriend others, and work away together.

see how it **GROWS.**

WHEN you GROW...
Things will happen at school, at home, at work, in your youth group, your student fellowship, women's meetings, midweek meetings, churches, communities, and so on.

You'll be **REACHING THROUGH TEACHING.**

WHEN you PRAY...
Remember those involved in writing and production of the study courses: pray for missionaries and nationals working on the translations into many different languages. Pray for groups studying that each member will not only be enriched personally, but will be reaching out continually to involve others. Pray for group leaders and those who direct the studies locally, nationally and internationally.

WHEN you PAY...
Realize that all profits from sales of studies go to develop the ministry on our mission fields and beyond, pay translators, and so on, and have the joy of knowing you are working together with them in the task.

INTRODUCTORY STUDY

The Gospel of John has been aptly described as: 'A pool in which a child may wade and an elephant may swim.' Perhaps more than any other book in the Bible, it is both simple and profound; simple enough to feed new believers, yet deep enough to keep scholars probing its depths without a sign of abatement. On average, a new work on this Gospel appears almost every year.

The Gospels of Matthew, Mark and Luke are called synoptic (i.e. broadly speaking seen through the same eyes) but John's book is different in many ways. The first three outline events which took place in Galilee (except for the Passion Story). John's Gospel centres around Jerusalem. Yet the accounts do not contradict each other and their stories can be interwoven without difficulty.

* * *

John writes as if to answer the question, 'Jesus Christ – Who is He?'

He does this in four ways:

1. By straight teaching as in chapter one.
2. By showing how people who met Jesus realised the truth – see chapter four.
3. By quoting Jesus' own words about Himself – see chapter eight.
4. By leaving us to draw our own conclusions from the stated facts.

As a result this one book is:

1. The evangelists' aid to point people to Christ the Lamb, the Shepherd, the Bread of Life, etc.
2. The best nourishment a new Christian can obtain.
3. An inexhaustible store house for the mature Christian.
4. A source of strength and comfort to many who are about to move on to their Father's House of many mansions.

Pray that this study in John's Gospel will challenge and strengthen you as it has done for millions since John was first inspired to write it.

When Jesus asked the disciples, 'Who do people say the Son of Man is?', He got a variety of answers.

Today if you asked a cross-section of people, 'Who is Jesus?', you would get many different answers.

How would you answer those who said the following?

'Jesus was a very impressive teacher, but I can't agree He was any greater than Buddha, Confucius or Socrates.'

'Wasn't Jesus a Superstar, or Superman? He was a myth they wrote a musical about.'

'I believe Jesus was a good man – possibly the best who ever lived.'

'He was the victim of a cruel conspiracy and it was dreadful the way they got Him in the end.'

'Jesus? Oh, a historical figure, full of "goodwill and peace on earth" and all that. But I don't see that He has any relevance for us today.'

* * *

Look up these references and see what Jesus claimed about Himself: John 8:42-47; John 14:6,10,11; Mark 14:61- 62.

Read what His enemies said about Him: John 5:18; John 7:15,20; John 10:33; John 18:38.

Learn, according to John, why He came to earth: John 3:16; John 10:10.

'John shows us Jesus, not as a figure of ancient history, but as the Eternal Contemporary, the Light of the World, the only True and living Way, now, as in John's day, to God' (A. M. Hunter).

LIVING PROOF

The people in these two dialogues are real people and the incidents actually happened.

I = Interviewer   H = Helen   S = Sonny

ONE

I: Good evening, Helen. You are a second year medical student I believe?

H: That's right.

I: And are you enjoying your course?

H: Oh, yes, I love it even more now.

I: Even more now? Wasn't it too good at first?

H: Well, my first six months at University were great. I made lots of friends and found life pleasant. I prided myself in my practical, no-nonsense approach to life. I knew about Christianity because a close school friend used to talk to me of her faith in Christ.

I: Did you become a Christian at school then?

H: Oh no. As far as I was concerned there were too many obstacles to belief. I felt if I let God into my life I'd lose my identity. I didn't want to become a meek-and-mild churchgoer!

I: That's interesting. Yet now you are a Christian. How did the change come about?

H: One night last year I opened my old school Bible. I can't explain why. I read at random in the Gospel of John and the words seemed to bounce off the page and hit me. They spoke of a grain of wheat dying and becoming many more grains. In a strange way I knew I was reading the truth. A few nights later, sitting alone by the fire, I began to realise the truth about MYSELF. I saw that my life had no direction because I was living for myself alone. At last, I knew that my belief was important and that I could no longer live my life on my own terms. Quietly, but with a sense of relief and freedom, I committed my life to God and to His service.

I: And you haven't regretted that decision?

H: Certainly not! That was nine months ago, and life is just so terrific. I know that God loves me and I just want to tell everybody about Jesus – to shout the message of His love and forgiveness from the rooftops.

(Adapted from Encounter magazine)

TWO

I: Good evening, Sonny. I think you too have reason to praise God for John's Gospel haven't you?

S: Yes, indeed! A verse in chapter 20 changed my whole life.

I: Will you tell us about it?

S: Certainly. I am an Indian from South Africa and was brought up a Hindu. When I first heard the gospel I was amazed that God loved me. I was drawn to the Lord Jesus, but could not yield because my loyalty to Hinduism was so strong.

I: That must have been a difficult position to be in.

S: It was. I was so torn apart with the conflict that one day I challenged Jesus saying, 'If you are real show yourself to me'.

I: And did He?

S: My challenge was met sooner than I expected. The following Saturday I was invited to a film show. To my surprise the film was about someone with the same problem as I had. His name was Thomas. He wanted to see Jesus too. I said, 'This is great. I've asked for the same thing'.

I: Well, Jesus did appear to Thomas didn't He? But that was 2,000 years ago when Jesus lived on earth. Did you really expect to see Him like Thomas did?

S: Yes, I did. But then I heard those words from John's Gospel and they had a dramatic effect on me. Jesus said to Thomas, 'Have you believed because you have seen Me? Happy are those who have not seen yet believe'. In a flash I understood that to believe His Word is to see the reality of His TRUTH.

I: And now you are here in Australia, Sonny. Why?

S: I'm at Bible College. I want to learn how to tell others that they too can believe that Jesus is the Son of God, and that believing, they can have LIFE through His Name.

STUDY 1

QUESTIONS

DAY 1 John 1:1-13; Colossians 1:15-18.
a) What is the relationship between Jesus (the Word) and the world?

b) How does a person become a true child of God (v. 12)?

DAY 2 Compare John 1:14-28 with 1 John 4:1-3; 1 Timothy 3:16 and Philippians 2:6-7.
a) What important reason for the Incarnation (that is, the Word becoming flesh) is given in John 1:18? There is another in Colossians 1:20.

b) Can you put into your own words the comparison John the Baptist drew between Jesus and himself?

DAY 3 John 1:29-34.
a) What convinced John the Baptist that Jesus was the Son of God?

b) Exodus 12:21-23; Isaiah 53:7-8. Which verse in today's reading from John links in with these verses?

c) As Lamb, what would happen to Jesus?

DAY 4 John 1:35-51.
a) In what different ways did these five men come to meet Jesus?

b) What new titles do Andrew and Nathaniel give Jesus?

DAY 5   John 2:1-12.
   a) What wise advice did Mary give to the servants?

   b) What was special about this miracle?

   c) This miracle is called a 'sign' in some translations. Why is it called this (John 20:30-31)?

DAY 6   John 2:13-25.
   a) The religious leaders in Jerusalem could have used Jesus' action here to destroy Him. What sign would demonstrate His right to do these things?

   b) Who are God's temple today (1 Cor. 3:16-17; 6:19-20; 1 Pet. 2:5)? What responsibilities are attached to these privileges?

DAY 7   John 3:1-6.
   a) Nicodemus was both right and wrong about Jesus. Discuss.

   b) Why is a NEW birthday absolutely essential for everyone (Rom. 8:8-9)?

NOTES

THE GOSPELS
Each Gospel starts uniquely:

MATTHEW writes as a Jew for his own people and so traces our Lord's ancestry back to Abraham via King David.

LUKE writes as a Gentile for all mankind and so traces Christ's ancestry back to Adam.

MARK begins with 'the gospel about Jesus Christ, the Son of God,' introducing us to the Lord, now 30 years old, in Galilee.

JOHN takes us right back into eternity, 'In the beginning was the Word'.

THE WORD was the Jewish synonym for God (Ps. 33:6). Gentiles also used the term, meaning 'Creator of all things'. The term therefore has significance when used in reference to Jesus Christ the Son of God. He is the Word who 'became flesh and made his dwelling among us. We have seen his glory, the glory of the One and Only, who came from the Father, full of grace and truth'.

JOHN AND THE FIRST DISCIPLES Chapter 1:19-51.
John the Baptist (as distinct from John, the writer of this Gospel) is the last of the prophets and the greatest man of his age. Here we see him being totally eclipsed by his cousin, Jesus. John readily bows to this and encourages his followers to go after the One greater than himself. John gives fuller details here than the other Gospels do, showing how Peter, John and Andrew came to be involved with Jesus before He called them from fishing to become 'fishers of men'.

THE FIRST SIGN Chapter 2:1-12.
The miracle of water made wine! The arrival of Jesus and His new friends may have contributed to the shortage. Perhaps that is why Mary felt responsible and turned to Him for help.

CLEANSING THE TEMPLE Chapter 2:13-21.
Jesus' challenge to the temple authorities cut across a lucrative source of income for the High Priest and his family. It was a blatant case of using religious scruples as an excuse for profit. Jesus repeated this challenge just before the crucifixion. We can well understand why those in authority were continually watching for opportunities to find fault with Him.

Two good verses to memorise – Chapter 1:12 and 1:29.

STUDY 2

QUESTIONS

DAY 1 John 3:7-15.
a) Why is the wind a good illustration of the work of the Spirit of God?

b) Numbers 21:4-9. How does this incident compare with Jesus' death on the cross?

DAY 2 John 3:16-21.
a) What do these verses tell us about the life that comes to us through the Lord Jesus Christ?

b) Why are people judged and condemned (vv. 18-19)?

DAY 3 John 3:22-36.
a) What great qualities are revealed in John the Baptist?

b) How is Jesus described in verse 34?

c) Why is it important to believe in Jesus (v. 36)?

DAY 4 John 4:1-15.
a) What indicates the humanity of Jesus in this story?

b) How did Jesus gain the woman's confidence? (Notice how His approach was different from that used with Nicodemus.)

c) How is the water that Jesus gives described (v. 10)? What was special about it?

DAY 5   John 4:16-26.
a) Discuss how the woman tried to dodge the moral probing here.

b) What did Jesus say about worship in verse 23? (Have you thought out the difference between religion and true worship?)

c) Who did Jesus claim to be (vv. 25-26)?

DAY 6   John 4:27-42.
a) What two matters were puzzling the disciples?

b) What important lessons does Jesus teach about Christian service?

c) What two things convinced the Samaritans that they should believe (vv. 39-41)? What title did they give Jesus?

DAY 7   John 4:43-54.
a) How do we know that news of Jesus' miracles was already widespread?

b) In what ways were the experiences of the royal official and the Samaritans similar?

NOTES

THE FIRST DISCUSSION – JESUS AND NICODEMUS TALK ABOUT THE NEW BIRTH Chapter 3.

Jesus' example as a personal worker should be noticed. He met Nicodemus on the point of his perplexity. Although a Pharisee, a teacher, and probably a leading teacher at that time, Nicodemus did not have the answer. Jesus zeroed right in and told him he needed NEW LIFE – a SPIRITUAL REBIRTH. John 3:16 is a key verse to memorise. Do you know it? Have you experienced it?

THE SECOND DISCUSSION – JESUS AND THE WOMAN TALK ABOUT LIVING WATER Chapter 4.

She came for water. She needed water. Jesus asked her for a drink. Simply, naturally, He made her realise her spiritual thirst was much more acute than her physical need. The living water He offered her was the spiritual life He alone can give (John 7:37-39). The woman's response was instantaneous. Her witness was clear and unhesitating. Why do some people respond quickly to the Lord? Why do our prayers for others often seem to go unheeded? It seems Nicodemus did not change until he saw Christ on the cross. We need to learn to watch as well as pray to have patience while God, by His Spirit, works in hearts.

THE SECOND SIGN – A BOY IS HEALED Chapter 4.

John alone records the healing of the royal official's son. The healing took place at a distance and in response to the earnest request of one who had simple faith in Jesus and reacted in obedience to His word.

Good verses to memorise – John 3:7, 16, 30; 4:13, 14.

STUDY 3

QUESTIONS

DAY 1   John 5:1-18.
a) What demand did Jesus make of the man healed here (v. 14)? Does He make the same demand of us (Rom. 6:1-2)?

b) Why were the Jews antagonistic to Jesus?

DAY 2   John 5:19-27.
a) What two prerogatives of God does Jesus claim as His?

b) What two conditions are set for those who would receive eternal life (v. 24)?

DAY 3   John 5:28-40.
a) Compare verses 24 and 29. Who can we say are those who do good and share in resurrection life?

b) What four witnesses does Jesus refer to as evidence that He has come from God (vv. 33, 36, 37, 39)?

DAY 4   John 5:41-47.
a) What did Jesus accuse the Jews of? Could we be accused of the same?

b) Would you say the Lord valued the Old Testament? Do you?

DAY 5   John 6:1-27.
   a) Why were these people attracted to Jesus in the first place (v. 2)?

   b) What made Him even more attractive to them?

   c) How did Jesus want them to react to this miracle?

DAY 6   John 6:28-40.
   a) How did Jesus answer the people's question in verse 28?

   b) What claims does Jesus make for Himself?

   c) What important promise does He give in verse 37?

DAY 7   John 6:41-59.
   a) How has Jesus compared the bread of life with the manna in the wilderness (also v. 30)?

   b) What do you think is meant here by eating His flesh and drinking His blood?

NOTES

THE THIRD SIGN – THE HEALING OF THE LAME MAN Chapter 5.
There was little in this man to endear him to anyone. Despite the protests, Jesus took the initiative and healed the man. He simply commanded. The man OBEYED and was immediately healed.

THE THIRD DISCUSSION – THE DIVINE SON.
This section may not be the best known of Jesus' messages, but it contains some of His richest words. He claims a unique relationship and equality of power with God the Father. This, coupled with His defiant act of healing on the Sabbath, added fuel to the fires of resentment already kindled at Jerusalem.

THE FOURTH SIGN – FEEDING THE MULTITUDE Chapter 6.
This is the only miracle, apart from the resurrection, recorded in all four Gospels. John gives us the extra details concerning Philip and Andrew and the boy with the loaves and fish. What is more important is the reaction which follows and this John gives in great detail.

THE FIFTH SIGN – WALKING ON THE WATER.
Matthew's Gospel gives this miracle in greater detail – also Mark. John does not elaborate but rather chooses to give fuller coverage to the discourse on the Bread of Life, which arises from the fourth sign, the feeding of the multitude.

THE FOURTH DISCUSSION – THE BREAD OF LIFE.
Look at 6:35. Here are some of the most memorable words of Jesus – also some of the most perplexing! The point of importance is that Jesus was seeking to move their interest from bodily to spiritual hunger and showing that He could meet every need they might have, if only they would trust Him. However, before these needs could be met, His body had to be broken and His blood shed on the cross.

Are you memorising these verses? John 5:24; 6:35, 37.

STUDY 4

QUESTIONS

DAY 1   John 6:60-71.
   a) What three reasons did Peter give for not forsaking Jesus (vv. 68-69)?

   b) What does Jesus offer throughout this chapter and why did the people fail to respond (v. 52)?

DAY 2   John 7:1-24.
   a) What kind of person discovers that Jesus teaches the truth (v. 17)?

   b) Jesus' opponents were using one of His miracles to condemn Him (v. 23). How does He show the hypocrisy of their charge?

DAY 3   John 7:25-53.
   a) The people came short of admitting Jesus was the Christ. What were their excuses for not doing so (vv. 27, 41, 42)?

   b) What did the temple guards who had been sent to arrest Jesus report about Him (v. 46)?

   c) In this chapter try and find titles that the people gave to Jesus and arrange them in ascending order.

DAY 4   John 8:1-11.
   a) In what way would Jesus offend both Roman authority and the Jews if He pronounced an assessment of this woman (John 18:31)?

b) Can you imagine why Jesus dealt so gently with the woman? How would the woman now view her sin in the light of His action?

c) Discuss the possible guidance Jesus' action gives for Christian workers.

DAY 5   John 8:12-29.
a) Why would Jesus' critics be unable to go where He was going (v. 21)?

b) What was going to happen before many would believe in Him (v. 28; John 3:14-15)?

DAY 6   John 8:30-59.
a) The Jews claimed they had freedom. What kind of freedom did Jesus offer (vv. 33-36)?

b) Pick out one statement of Jesus which clearly indicates that He claimed equality with God (Exod. 3:14)?

DAY 7   John 9:1-17.
a) How did this man explain the transformation that had taken place in his life? How did he now view Jesus (v. 17)?

b) Do these verses show that suffering need not necessarily be due to sin?

NOTES

THE FIFTH DISCUSSION – THE LIFE GIVING SPIRIT Chapter 7.
The Feast of Tabernacles was held in autumn to both mark the end of harvest and commemorate God's provision throughout Israel's wilderness journey. During the last day of the feast, Jesus broke in on the festivities to claim He would give LIVING WATER and much more. He was really speaking of the Holy Spirit who had not yet been given. The same truth came out in His discussion with the woman of Samaria at the well. He promised her that the water He would give her would so satisfy her that she would never thirst again. Here He says that the water would not only satisfy the individual, but that there would be enough to pass on in blessing to others.

THE INCIDENT IN THE TEMPLE Chapter 8.
Some modern translations place parentheses round this story or place it in another section of the book. This is because of divergence of opinion amongst the various manuscripts available to translators. However, since it does not interrupt the narrative in any way, it is best left in its traditional place in our study. It is a beautiful story perfectly illustrating Jesus' ability to make a sinful person suitably contrite while at the same time offering His forgiveness. The religious leaders meant it as a trap to catch Him out. He not only helped the woman, but sent His opponents away in disarray.

THE SIXTH DISCUSSION – THE LIGHT OF THE WORLD Chapter 9.
Here the discourse precedes the sign, possibly because both this and the Good Shepherd story bear on the healing of the blind man. It shows how His enemies were now in full array against Him, while Jesus was absolutely forthright in His accusations against them. They were deliberately rejecting TRUTH and fabricating all kinds of falsehoods against Him, preferring DARKNESS to LIGHT.

How is that memory work going? John 6:68; 7:37-38; 8:12; 8:58.

STUDY 5

QUESTIONS

DAY 1   John 9:18-41.
  a) Trace the development in the blind man's attitude to Jesus (vv. 11, 17, 33, 38).

  b) Discuss verse 39 in the light of John 12:47. How can both verses be true?

DAY 2   John 10:1-18.
  a) What did Jesus mean when He said, 'I am the gate' (v. 9)?

  b) What reason did Jesus give for His life and death? What shows that His death was not martyrdom?

DAY 3   John 10:19-30.
  a) How is a true follower of Jesus described (v. 27)?

  b) What promise does Jesus give to those who feel they 'can't make it' (vv. 28-29)?

  c) On what great claim does this promise rest (v. 30)?

DAY 4   John 10:31-42.
  a) What indicates that the Jews clearly understood that Jesus was claiming equality with God?

b) What does Jesus tell His critics to take note of as evidence that He did come from God?

c) Pick out some of the ways Jesus describes His relationship to His Father in this chapter.

DAY 5   John 11:1-16.
a) How could a delay in answered prayer be for the glory of God?

b) What supernatural insight had Jesus into Lazarus' situation?

DAY 6   John 11:17-27.
a) What three correct statements did Martha make about Jesus and His power?

b) Should the statement 'I am the resurrection and the life' make any difference to a Christian's attitude to life and death?

DAY 7   John 11:28-44.
a) What probably made the men remove the stone from the grave (v. 41)?

b) Why do you think Jesus prayed aloud?

NOTES

THE SIXTH SIGN – THE BLIND MAN HEALED Chapter 9.
Although similar stories are told in other Gospels, this man and the account here seem unique. The story fully demonstrates what Jesus had been saying about the blindness and prejudice of the Jewish leaders. They will not believe the man and they so terrify the parents that they cannot answer a simple question. When they banish the man from the temple, Jesus finds him and gives him a challenge to trust Him – which the man accepts. He has received both physical and spiritual sight! Now he can say, 'One thing I do know. I was blind, but now I see.' The Pharisees, who thought they had spiritual sight, are condemned as blind.

THE SEVENTH DISCUSSION – THE GOOD SHEPHERD Chapter 10.
Old Testament prophets such as Jeremiah and Ezekiel had spoken against the religious leaders of their day. They called them false shepherds because they cared more for themselves than their flock. Here Jesus draws a comparison between false shepherds and Himself, the Good Shepherd. He says, 'I am ... the gate (door)', 'I am ... the good shepherd.' His statements cause division among the Jews (v.19), but Jesus affirms, 'My sheep listen to my voice; I know them. I give them eternal life, and they shall never perish; no-one can snatch them out of my hand.'

THE SEVENTH SIGN – THE RAISING OF LAZARUS Chapter 11.
Here is another account peculiar to John's Gospel. Two other recorded instances of Jesus raising the dead are given in the story of Jairus' daughter and the Widow's son. Jesus delays His response to the sisters' message until eventually when He arrives at Bethany, Lazarus has been dead four days. This further miracle of raising Lazarus involves the Judaean leaders in further plotting and more specific plans for His downfall.

Jesus makes this tremendous statement: 'I am the Resurrection and the Life. He who believes in me ... will never die.'

More verses to hide in your heart: John 9:25; 10:9, 11, 27, 28; 11:25-26.

STUDY 6

QUESTIONS

DAY 1   John 11:45-57.
   a) Can you see that there was more truth in Caiaphas' statement than he realised (vv. 50-52)?

   b) What happened as a result of the Sanhedrin meeting?

DAY 2   John 12:1-11.
   a) What guidelines can you find here for worship and giving?

   b) Since the Sadducees did not believe in the resurrection of the dead, how would you imagine they would have reacted to the Lazarus incident?

DAY 3   John 12:12-19; Matthew 21:8; Mark 11:7; Luke 19:35.
   a) In this Palm Sunday story find an additional reason for the crowd's enthusiasm.

   b) What do you think the people meant in verse 13? Is there a greater meaning behind these words?

DAY 4   John 12:20-36.
   a) If verse 24 refers to Jesus' death, what is implied for His followers in verses 25-26?

b) What was causing confusion among the crowd (v. 34)?

DAY 5   John 12:37-50.
  a) What glimpse do we get into Christ's pre-existence and deity (v. 41; Isa. 6:1)?

  b) Discuss the various reactions of the people to the ministry of Jesus.

  c) Why is it so serious to reject Jesus (v. 48)?

DAY 6   John 13:1-17.
  a) Assuming the disciples had bathed before coming to supper, discuss the spiritual meaning of Jesus' words to Peter in verses 9-10.

  b) What example is set for us in verse 5 and Philippians 2:5-8?

DAY 7   John 13:18-30.
  a) Judas sat in a place of honour, close to Jesus, yet he betrayed Jesus. Is there a warning here for us?

  b) Discuss the connection between verse 30 and chapter 12:35-36.

NOTES

THE SUPPER AT BETHANY Chapter 12:1-10.
Martha, Mary and Lazarus are involved in a supper given in honour of Lazarus. Martha, as ever, is busy serving; Mary shows her devotion by a costly act of sacrifice; Lazarus brings honour by just being there, alive and well! Note that Lazarus is in danger of his life because of his association with Jesus.

PALM SUNDAY Chapter 12:12-19.
John gives a short version compared with the other Gospels, but he adds the details of those who knew of the raising of Lazarus and were testifying about the miracle to the crowd, thus adding a further note of rejoicing.

WE WOULD SEE JESUS Chapter 12:20-36.
Some Greeks ask Philip if they can see Jesus. This request evokes some great statements from the Lord, especially verse 32, 'But I, when I am lifted up from the earth, will draw all men to myself'. Here again we have a section of the Lord's words largely overlooked as this Gospel is read and yet they are some of His most searching statements.

WASHING THE DISCIPLES' FEET – THE LAST SUPPER – JUDAS' DEPARTURE Chapter 13:1-30.
We have no record here of the institution of the sacrament of Communion, but these events point to it. The incident of 'foot washing' occurred during the meal, but presumably before the final act of breaking the bread, etc. However, the identification of the betrayer at supper is given in some detail and the story shows how well Judas must have hidden his intentions. Following Judas' exit, Jesus gives to the remaining disciples some memorable teaching for their future service.

Two great verses to learn – John 12:24, 32.

STUDY 7

QUESTIONS

DAY 1   John 13:31-38.
   a) What mark of genuine discipleship is set out here (vv. 34-35)?

   b) John 14:15-17; Romans 5:5; Galatians 5:22. What relation is there between these verses and the command of Jesus in John 13:34?

DAY 2   John 14:1-6.
   a) Why were the disciples not to be troubled? Can this apply to us?

   b) Discuss the implications for us of Jesus being the Way, the Truth, and the Life.

DAY 3   John 14:7-11.
   a) People ask 'What is God like?' How does Jesus answer that puzzling question?

   b) Pick out one reason why we can trust Jesus.

DAY 4   John 14:12-17.
   a) The promises in verses 12-14 seem impossible at first reading. Is this because we have failed to believe Him? Can you think of examples proving that God keeps His promises?

   b) What is told us about the Holy Spirit in these verses?

DAY 5   John 14:18-26.
   a) In these verses and verse 15 find the test of our genuine love for the Lord.

   b) What more are we told about the Holy Spirit?

DAY 6   John 14:26-31.
   a) What present and future blessings are promised to the Christian here?

   b) What reason does Jesus give for His move out to Gethsemane (v. 31)?

DAY 7   John 15:1-10.
   a) What does dwelling, abiding or remaining in Christ mean? How can we do this?

   b) What results from abiding (vv. 5-7)?

NOTES

'DO NOT LET NOT YOUR HEARTS BE TROUBLED' Chapter 13:31 – 14:31.
After Judas has gone, Jesus tells His disciples that the time of His glory has come. Soon He will face the cross, rise from the dead and go to be with the Father. He gives them a NEW commandment: 'Love one another'.

Peter intervenes with a question and a bold assertion (vv. 36-37). Following His warning to Peter, the Lord goes on to speak words of comfort and assurance to them all (ch. 14). This chapter is packed full of promises!

'I am going there to prepare a place for you.'
'I will come back and take you to be with me.'
'I am the way and the truth and the life.'
'You may ask me for anything in my name, and I will do it.'
'I will ask the Father, and he will give you another Counsellor.'
'I will not leave you as orphans.'
'Because I live, you also will live.'
'Peace I leave with you; my peace I give you.'

THE TRUE VINE Chapter 15:1-10.
In the Old Testament Israel is often regarded as God's Vine or Vineyard, but so often Israel did not 'bear fruit' as God required. (The vine has absolutely no use apart from bearing fruit.) Here Jesus says He IS the True or Genuine Vine. His fruit can be guaranteed. While the branches are kept nourished by the vine they will bear fruit. In this we see a picture of the Christian's total dependence on Christ for life and fruitfulness. We have the converse too: without Christ we can do nothing. This portion is enriched by the repeated command to 'Love one another' which is the test of true discipleship.

Are you regularly adding to your list of memory verses? John 13:34; 14:3, 6, 14, 15, 27; 15:5, 7.

STUDY 8

QUESTIONS

DAY 1 John 15:11-19.
    a) What statement here should make us proud (in the right sense) and yet humble?

    b) Did Jesus save us simply to take us to heaven?

DAY 2 John 15:20-27.
    a) Who did Jesus say were guilty of sin and without excuse?

    b) Who would continue to witness when Jesus would have gone to His Father?

DAY 3 John 16:1-15.
    a) How do we know the disciples must have been depressed at what Jesus was saying?

    b) Jesus reveals further facts about the Holy Spirit's work. What are they?

DAY 4 John 16:16-33; Romans 8:26-27.
    a) Is there a difference between Christian joy and other sources of joy?

    b) Find the verses which should give us more confidence and guide us when we pray.

DAY 5   John 17:1-5.
          a) How is eternal life described?

          b) How had Jesus glorified His Father?

          c) What would His Father do?

DAY 6   John 17:6-19.
          a) Note the things that Jesus had done for the disciples.

          b) What special prayer does He offer for them?

DAY 7   John 17:20-26.
          a) How would others come to believe in Jesus?

          b) What special prayer does Jesus offer for all who will become
             Christians?

NOTES

THE HOLY SPIRIT

Jesus, alone with His disciples in the Upper Room, gives clear teaching about the Holy Spirit. The Greek word for the Spirit is 'Paraclete' which means 'Helper' or 'Advocate' – literally, the One who comes alongside to help, strengthen and encourage.

In chapter 14 Christ promises that the Spirit will come to the disciples. He will be WITH and IN them. He will TEACH them and help them REMEMBER what they had been taught.

In chapter 15 the Spirit will bear witness to the Lord Jesus Christ in and through the disciples.

In chapter 16 He is set forth as the One who will convince the world of sin, righteousness and judgement; the One who will guide them into truth and reveal the future. In all that He does He will glorify the Lord Jesus Christ.

These are all additional details to those given in chapters 2, 3 and 7. Now as He reveals the work that the Spirit will do following Christ's resurrection and ascension, Christians can be assured of the Spirit's presence, comfort, strengthening and enabling in any situation in which God places them. Surely it would be sheer folly to reject Christ and so put ourselves out of the sphere of His presence, peace and power. Although much of the Holy Spirit's work remains a mystery to us, we do know that His work is to glorify the Lord Jesus Christ. What Jesus taught us is simple enough and adequate for genuine Christian living.

CHAPTER 17

The Lord's Prayer - often called the High Priestly prayer because in it He intercedes for His people. It covered not only the Christians of His day, but us as well. We see in it Christ's heart yearning over His own. What a privilege to know He still prays for us (Hebrews 7:25; Romans 8:34). Did you notice that unlike us, Jesus did not have to pray for personal forgiveness and cleansing? This testifies to His Divine Nature.

Are you still memorising? – John 15:16; John 16:33; John 17:3, 15.

STUDY 9

QUESTIONS

DAY 1 John 18:1-11.
  a) Which verses indicate that Jesus was in control, and not a victim of circumstances?

  b) Who did the soldiers and officials say they were looking for (vv. 4-5)?

  c) Jesus said: 'I am he' (compare Exod. 3:14). Can you remember other titles Jesus claimed for Himself in this Gospel (e.g. 6:35)?

DAY 2 John 18:12-27.
  a) Why might Peter have been really afraid here?

  b) What outstanding qualities of character does Jesus manifest before the High Priest and his colleagues?

DAY 3 John 18:28-40.
  a) What had Jesus consistently said about His death (John 3:14-15; 8:28; 12:32-34)? How did the Jewish leaders unwittingly help fulfil this declaration?

  b) What did Jesus say about truth before Pilate?

DAY 4 John 19:1-16.
  a) Trace Pilate's attempts to avoid condemning Jesus. What finally broke his resistance (18:31, 39; 19:6, 12)?

b) How do you imagine Barabbas must have felt if he saw Jesus on the cross?

c) Pilate 'sat down on the judge's seat' (v. 13). When we pass judgment on Jesus who really is being judged?

DAY 5   John 19:17-37.
a) What prophecies in Psalm 22:14-18 were fulfilled in the crucifixion of Jesus?

b) Read Isaiah 53:4-12 prayerfully and thank the Lord for all He suffered for your sake.

DAY 6   John 19:38-42.
a) What risk were Joseph and Nicodemus taking?

b) In view of their lavish gifts, what did they NOT expect to happen?

DAY 7   John 20:1-10.
a) How do these verses show that Mary was not anticipating the resurrection?

b) What did John see that made him believe?

NOTES

ARREST Chapter 18:1-10.
John's story omits details of Jesus' agony in the garden while the disciples slept, but it highlights Judas' treachery and the vain defence put up by Peter.

TRIAL Chapter 18:12-24.
Christ's trials before Annas and Caiaphas can be seen to be a mockery of justice, but were a necessary prelude to the official trial before Pilate.

DENIAL Chapter 18:15-27.
John tells the story briefly so that possibly he can link it up with Peter's restitution which comes at the end of the Gospel. An interesting detail he does give is the first question (v. 17) which is phrased in the original in such a way that 'No' would be the automatic answer. We would say: 'Surely YOU aren't one of HIS disciples?"

PILATE Chapter 18:28 – 19:22.
Pilate was what might be called a self-made man and so was clinging to power by a very fine thread. He had made many rash mistakes in Judea already and could not afford to blunder again. The Emperor in Rome would rather depose Pilate than risk perpetual riots in his province. The other Gospels indicate that Pilate's wife knew something of Jesus, and the Jews who had been plotting against Him for many months may have influenced Pilate too. The very presence of our Lord himself drove Pilate back to his basic conviction of Roman justice. However, the perpetual threats from the Jews finally broke him down.

CRUCIFIXION Chapter 19:17-42.
John was an eyewitness (v. 6) and does not linger on the terrible scene, except to show that it was no accident, but according to the Scriptures and God's total plan for our Redemption.

EASTER MORNING Chapter 20:1-10.
Note how the two secret disciples, Joseph and Nicodemus, come forward now when all hope seems to have vanished. Joseph provides the tomb, he and Nicodemus an abundance of spices for preserving the body, while Mary, after waiting till the end of the Sabbath, comes to the tomb to complete the embalming.

A vital memory verse – John 19:30.

STUDY 10

Questions

DAY 1 John 20:11-18.
> a) John must have been the first to believe that Jesus had risen but what were the two special 'firsts' for Mary?
>
> b) Jesus tells Mary not to touch Him. Why might He have said this when later He invited the disciples to do so (Luke 24:39; John 20:17)?

DAY 2 John 20:19-23.
> a) What further proof do we have that the Jesus who died was the same Jesus who had been resurrected?
>
> b) What were the disciples commissioned to do?

DAY 3 John 20:24-31.
> a) Thomas makes a complete avowal of faith here. What titles does he give to Jesus?
>
> b) How can someone who has not seen the risen Lord come to trust in Him?

DAY 4 John 21:1-8.
> a) Can you think why these disciples went back to the old way of life?
>
> b) Discuss what they may have learned from this experience.

DAY 5   John 21:9-14.
   a) What does the Lord Jesus reveal here about Himself?

   b) What does this meal with the disciples remind you of?

DAY 6   John 21:15-19.
   a) Why do you think Jesus asked Peter three times to affirm his love
   for Him?

   b) How does 1 Peter 5:1-5 confirm that Peter obeyed the Lord?

DAY 7   John 21:20-25.
   a) Try to put verses 21 and 22 into your own words.

   b) Does this portion teach you anything specific about the Lord's
   plans for you and for others?

NOTES

JESUS IS ALIVE: MARY SEES JESUS Chapter 20:11-18.
John had seen that Jesus must have risen from the tomb, but it was Mary who first saw the risen Lord. Mary Magdalene had been delivered from demon possession and was a loyal follower of the Lord. She had been almost the last at the cross and is now first at the tomb and first to see Him alive. Her loyalty was rewarded and she was given the priceless privilege of going and telling the others the good news that she had seen the risen Lord.

THE DISCIPLES AND THOMAS Chapter 20:19-29.
Jesus now appears to the disciples where they are all gathered together with the exception of Thomas. His absence is not explained, but he has to wait another week before his doubts are dispelled. Once he is convinced, Thomas is privileged to make the greatest recorded acknowledgement of Christ in the Gospel: 'My Lord and my God'.

AT THE SEA OF GALILEE Chapter 20:30 and Chapter 21.
Jesus appears just when Peter and his friends are discouraged at having caught no fish. Following His instructions, as on an earlier occasion, they have a huge catch. John recognises Jesus from the boat, but Peter dives in to swim to Him. Then comes the threefold challenge to Peter and he is given the chance to return to His Master's service, this time as a shepherd.
There seems to be a double ending to this Gospel. At verses 30 and 31 of chapter 20 the AIM of the book is given, showing why the book has been used so powerfully down the centuries to point people to the Saviour. In chapter 21:25 there is a second conclusion, which simply and surely emphasises the glorious Person and Work of the One of whom John has written.

Some wonderful final memory verses – John 20:28, 29, 31.

ANSWER GUIDE

The following pages contain an Answer Guide. It is recommended that answers to the questions be attempted before turning to this guide. It is only a guide and the answers given should not be treated as exhaustive.

GUIDE TO STUDY 1

DAY 1

a) Creator of everything, its true life and light. He was neither received nor recognised by those whom He had created.

b) By receiving the Lord Jesus and putting our trust in Him. (More of this in chapter 3.)

DAY 2

a) No man has ever seen God, but Jesus in the flesh was a revelation of God to us. Jesus took on bodily form in order to die as our Saviour and thus reconcile us to God.

b) John acknowledges Jesus as pre-existent to him and greater in every way. He considered himself unworthy of the most menial service and only 'a voice' preparing the way for Christ's coming.

DAY 3

a) The fulfilment of God's promise of the Holy Spirit descending on Jesus like a dove convinced John and brought the declaration that He was the Son of God.

b) Verse 29: the Old Testament readings refer to a lamb.

c) He would die on behalf of others. This pointed forward to His death on the cross.

DAY 4

a) Andrew and John went to Jesus at John the Baptist's bidding; Peter was introduced to Him by his brother Andrew; Jesus Himself found Philip; Philip introduced Nathaniel to Jesus.

b) The Messiah (Christ); Rabbi; King of Israel.

DAY 5

a) To obey Jesus in everything they were told to do.

b) It was Jesus' first miracle.

c) John sees the miracle as demonstrating who Jesus Christ really was, the Son of God, and not simply as the mere exercise of power.

DAY 6

    a) The sign would be His own resurrection which would declare Him as the Son of God (Rom. 1:4). As such He had the right to defend His Father's House.

    b) Individual believers and church fellowships. Each one should be 'on guard' to ensure that God's name is not dishonoured.

DAY 7

    a) He rightly assessed that Jesus must have come from God to be able to work miracles. He underestimated who Jesus was by merely calling Him 'Rabbi' – teacher.

    b) The New Birth ensures Eternal Life. To miss the New Birth results in eternal death.

GUIDE TO STUDY 2

DAY 1

    a) We do not see the wind, but we can see the results of its presence. So with the work of the Holy Spirit – we can see the changes He produces in the lives of God's children.

    b) In each case the condition for life was the look of faith.

DAY 2

    a) Jesus Christ imparts to every believer the life of God Himself.

    b) People condemn themselves when they choose darkness (the way of evil) and refuse to believe in Jesus.

DAY 3

    a) Honesty; humility; great generosity.

    b) He speaks God's words and is fully anointed with the Holy Spirit.

    c) Believing in Him leads to eternal life; rejection of Him leads to eternal death.

DAY 4

    a) Jesus was tired and probably thirsty (v. 4). What He had learned in verse 3 appears to have come about through natural means.

    b) He aroused her curiosity by asking for a drink and then developed the conversation naturally along the line of water.

    c) As 'living water'. It eliminates thirst completely and leads to eternal life.

DAY 5

    a) She tried to veer off on a theological tangent about where to worship!

    b) God desires it, but it must be done in spirit and in truth.

    c) The Messiah (Christ).

DAY 6

    a) Why He was talking to this woman and why He wasn't hungry.

    b) Christian witness and service know no barriers of class or race. Genuine devotion to service can make us forget about normal bodily appetites. Opportunities for service exist now.

    c) The woman's testimony and hearing the Lord Jesus personally. Saviour of the world (v. 42).

DAY 7

    a) The Galileans welcomed Him and the royal official came to meet Him.

    b) They both had heard of Jesus and came to Him; both believed in Him.

GUIDE TO STUDY 3

DAY 1

    a) He told him to stop sinning.
       Yes.

    b) This miracle had taken place on the Sabbath, and the Jews understood that when Jesus claimed God as His own Father He was making Himself equal with God.

DAY 2

    a) The ability to give life and to judge men.

    b) To listen to Jesus' word and believe in God.

DAY 3

    a) Only those who believe in the Lord Jesus Christ.

    b) John; Jesus' own works; the Father; the Scriptures.

DAY 4

    a) Of not loving God or seeking praise from Him alone; not believing what Moses had written.
       Personal, but it is easy for us to do the same.

    b) The Old Testament bore witness to Jesus. He accepted it as true and it was the groundwork on which He built. We cannot give it a lesser place than He did.

DAY 5

    a) They had seen marvellous works of healing.

    b) The miracle of the loaves and fish.

    c) He wanted them to believe in Him.

DAY 6

    a) Believe, trust in God.

    b) He is the bread of life who gives complete satisfaction; He is doing the Father's will; He raises those who believe in Him to resurrection life.

    c) He does not turn away anyone who comes to Him.

DAY 7

    a) The bread of life (the true bread) when eaten gives eternal life; those who ate the manna still eventually died.

    b) It certainly cannot be taken in a literal sense and is obviously a reference to the death of Jesus. We reap the benefits of Christ's death when we believe in Him.

GUIDE TO STUDY 4

DAY 1

    a) There was no one else to turn to; He alone had the message of eternal life; He was the Christ, Son of the living God.

    b) The bread of life (eternal life). They could not see beyond literal bread and physical hunger.

DAY 2

    a) The person who desires to do God's will is given spiritual discernment to know the truth.

    b) They were doing 'work' on the Sabbath in order to circumcise. Jesus was simply carrying out a work of mercy in making the man completely whole.

DAY 3

    a) They knew where He came from; they imagined no one would know where the Christ would come from. (Mistakenly, they thought He came from Galilee, but Jesus had come from Bethlehem.)

    b) That no one had ever spoken the way He did.

    c) Some said he was 'demon-possessed' (v. 20); others said: 'that man' (v. 11); 'good man' (v. 12); 'the Prophet' (v. 40); 'the Christ' (v. 41).

DAY 4

    a) He would offend Rome if He pronounced a sentence of death and offend the Jews if He did not.

    b) The woman had been so shamed by these men that Jesus saw that kindness and gentleness would lead her to repentance. She would see her sin as an offence not only against the Law but also against God's love.

    c) In counselling, compassion and righteousness need to be held in balance (v. 11).

DAY 5

    a) If they persisted in unbelief they would die in their sins and so miss eternal life and heaven.

    b) He was to be 'lifted up' (John 3:14-15; John 12:32-33).

DAY 6

    a) Jesus offered them freedom from the bondage of sin.

    b) Verse 58: God declared Himself the great 'I am'. Jesus did the same.

DAY 7

    a) To him it was simple: Jesus had put mud on his eyes, he had washed and now he could see.
    As a prophet.

    b) Many are born with disabilities certainly not due to their own sin. God may have hidden purposes in suffering which we cannot detect (v. 3).

GUIDE TO STUDY 5

DAY 1

    a) He called Him Jesus, then prophet, then man of God, then Lord.

    b) Jesus came to save, not to judge. But the person who rejects the light is judged; the person who receives the light is saved.

DAY 2

    a) The picture is probably drawn from the Eastern custom of the shepherds sleeping across the sheepfold entrance to prevent sheep from straying or intruders from entering. Jesus guards and protects us from evil when we put ourselves in His care.

    b) That His sheep might have life (v. 10).
    Jesus predicted His death; He deliberately said He would die of His own volition for His sheep.

DAY 3

 a) As someone who listens to Jesus and follows Him.
 b) Jesus knows those who belong to Him; no one who is saved by God's grace can be snatched from the hand of Jesus (v. 28), or His Father (v. 29).
 c) Jesus clearly states that He and the Father are one.

DAY 4

 a) They were ready to stone him.
 b) The works that He has done.
 c) See verses 15, 17, 25, 30, 32.

DAY 5

 a) A greater miracle would bring more glory to God. Delay also gives time to be sure that one is praying in the will of God. Once we are sure of this we can patiently wait for God to work (Rom. 8:28).
 b) He knew Lazarus had died.

DAY 6

 a) See verses 21, 22, 27.
 b) It should. Christians have eternal life now and physical death cannot destroy this.

DAY 7

 a) Jesus had told them to do this (v. 39). He spoke with authority and they probably were also naturally curious to know what He would do.
 b) As a further evidence that He came from God, and that God worked in response to prayer.

GUIDE TO STUDY 6

DAY 1

 a) The Lord's death was for the sin of the whole world (John 1:29).
 b) The Jewish leaders were determined to see Jesus arrested and killed.

DAY 2

 a) Jesus is worthy of the best we can give. No one should criticise those who worship God with the highest motive. James 2:15-18 indicates that we will consider the physical need of others if our spiritual witness to them is to be effective.
 b) Personal.

DAY 3

    a) The raising of Lazarus was becoming more widely known.

    b) The people saw Jesus as an earthly king coming to reign immediately in Jerusalem. In fact, He is King of Kings reigning over all who accept Him and submit to His rule.

DAY 4

    a) Similar suffering and, if necessary, death. We gain eternal life and honour from the Father through following Jesus.

    b) Their misconception that if He were the Christ then He would never die, and the title 'Son of Man'.

DAY 5

    a) The glory and title 'Lord' of Isaiah 6:1 is said to have been possessed by the Lord Jesus.

    b) Some refused to believe; others became 'secret' believers.

    c) To reject Jesus is to reject God's offer of reconciliation and to bring upon oneself condemnation.

DAY 6

    a) All the disciples had experienced Christ's inner cleansing except Judas, who rejected it. A Christian needs continual daily cleansing from sin.

    b) The example of humility in the service of others. Jesus was prepared to do the most menial task.

DAY 7

    a) It is possible to appear spiritual yet, like Judas, be shallow and superficial. There is a warning to be watchful in our spiritual walk (1 Cor. 10:12).

    b) Not only was Judas' dastardly action done in the darkness of night, but he chose a path of spiritual darkness which led to despair and eternal darkness.

GUIDE TO STUDY 7

DAY 1

    a) Love one another as the Lord has loved us.

    b) They speak of love. We can only love as the Holy Spirit enables us.

DAY 2

    a) Jesus would go, but would come back for them; in His absence He would be acting on their behalf.

This applies to all who trust in God and in the Lord Jesus.
b) He not only shows us the way to God – He is the WAY.
He not only tells us the truth about God – He is the TRUTH.
He not only points us to life – He is LIFE, God's eternal life.
Jesus is unique. Eternal salvation is found in Him alone.

DAY 3

a) He said that those who had seen Him had seen the Father, so God is like Jesus.
b) The evidence of the miracles (Matt. 11:1-6).

DAY 4

a) Jesus' works took place in a limited geographical situation. But since then He has done marvellous deeds through His followers all over the world and through successive generations by the operation of the Spirit.
b) He is the Spirit of truth; Counsellor; He indwells a Christian.

DAY 5

a) Keeping and obeying His commands and teaching.
b) He is a divine teacher, the One who reminds us of Jesus' words.

DAY 6

a) Present: the presence of the Holy Spirit, peace. Future: the coming again of the Lord and the glories of heaven.
b) To show His love for His Father and His obedience to Him.

DAY 7

a) Keeping close contact with Him through prayer, Bible reading, fellowship and obedience to His word.
b) As we abide our prayers will be answered and our lives will show forth the fruits of His presence (Gal. 5:22-23).

GUIDE TO STUDY 8

DAY 1

a) Jesus had told His disciples all that His Father had made known to Him, and calls them His friends. We are His friends too if we belong to Him.

b) No; we are to bear fruit. This can mean bringing others to Jesus or becoming more like Him every day.

DAY 2

a) Those who had heard Him (v. 22) and had witnessed the miracles (v. 24).

b) The Holy Spirit (v. 26) and His disciples (v. 27).

DAY 3

a) Jesus refers to their grief (v. 6). They seemed too overwhelmed with sadness to even ask where He was going (v. 5).

b) The Spirit will convict the world of sin, righteousness and judgment. He will reveal the truth and future to them. In all of this He will glorify Jesus.

DAY 4

a) The Christian's joy comes from his eternal relationship with Christ and is not dependent upon people and circumstances. Other joys are fleeting and variable. The world can neither give nor take away the joy of Christ.

b) Verses 23, 24, 27.

DAY 5

a) As knowing God and Jesus Christ (v. 3).

b) Through His obedient accomplishing of the work God had given Him to do (v. 4).

c) Despite the shame of the cross, God would glorify Jesus (vv. 1, 5). He would be honoured in His presence. The resurrection and the ascension place Jesus at God's right hand, thus bestowing on Him His pre-incarnate glory (John 17:5).

DAY 6

a) Revealed God to them (v. 6); given them God's words (v. 8); kept and guarded them (v. 12); commissioned them (v. 18).

b) That they would be: united as one (v. 11); protected from the evil one (v. 15); sanctified by truth (v. 17).

DAY 7
- a) Through their witness (v. 20).
- b) He prayed for unity among them and that they would be with Him (in heaven) and see His glory.
- c) Glory. Authority over all people. Eternal life. The disciples. God's word, the same word He had received from the Father. The same glory that God had given Him.

GUIDE TO STUDY 9

DAY 1
- a) Verses 4, 11.
- b) Jesus of Nazareth.
- c) John 6:35; 8:12, 24, 28; 10:7, 11; 11:25; 14:6; 15:1.

DAY 2
- a) Most probably of being ridiculed or thought odd, or of reprisals at having cut off the servant's ear.
- b) Courage, confidence and composure.

DAY 3
- a) That He would be 'lifted up', that is, He would die on a cross.
  The Jewish leaders insisted that He be judged by Pilate as Jewish execution was stoning to death while Roman execution was crucifixion.
- b) Jesus said He testified to the truth and those on the side of truth listened to Him.

DAY 4
- a) He first tried to get the Jews to try Him by their law; then to release Him as a Passover dispensation. He insisted on Jesus' innocence.
  His resistance finally broke when the Jews accused him of being disloyal to Caesar.
- b) Barabbas must have known that Jesus was dying in his place.
- c) Ourselves. We are shown to be who we really are: sinners and incapable of making the right choices.

DAY 5
- a) The physical agony; evil men around Him; gambling for His clothes.
- b) How can anyone dare spurn such agony and love outpoured on his/her behalf?

DAY 6
  a) They ran the risk of social ostracism and ridicule. They would not be able to observe the Passover. Their future in the Sanhedrin would probably be jeopardised.
  b) They were not expecting Jesus to rise from the dead.

DAY 7
  a) She thought that Jesus' body had been stolen.
  b) What he saw inside the empty tomb: grave robbers would certainly not have left the grave clothes neatly folded and in position as though the body had passed through them.

GUIDE TO STUDY 10

DAY 1
  a) Mary was the first to see the risen Christ and the first to tell others that He was risen.
  b) There could be several reasons. He was alive, of that she had no doubt, so she did not have to touch Him to prove it. As the word used is to 'cling' rather than touch, Jesus may have been indicating that each had to be moving to the next destination; she could not keep Him forever. The words, 'I have not yet returned to the Father', may imply more opportunities of seeing Him.

DAY 2
  a) Jesus showed them His hands and side (where the nails obviously had been).
  b) To go in obedience to Jesus, in the power of the Holy Spirit.

DAY 3
  a) Lord and God.
  b) Primarily through the revelation of Jesus Christ as given in the Bible. Christians witness to what they read about in the Bible.

DAY 4
  a) Having temporarily lost the perpetual presence of the Lord it would be natural to gravitate back to their old life.
  b) They would realise the Lord had something far greater for them and that the old life was not for them.

DAY 5

    a) He showed clearly that He understands and will meet our needs both the simplest and the greatest.

    b) Personal: perhaps the feeding of the multitude with the loaves and fish or the Last Supper when Jesus ate with the disciples.

DAY 6

    a) Peter had previously denied the Lord three times.

    b) He later encouraged his contemporaries and Christian leaders of future generations to shepherd 'God's flock' as Jesus had commanded him (21:17).

DAY 7

    a) See the wording in various Bible translations.

    b) Our main concern should be to do God's will for our lives. It also teaches us that He is in control and therefore we must not presume we know better than He does; also, that we should be patient and rely on His perfect timing.

GEARED FOR GROWTH BIBLE STUDIES

- Have a daily encounter with God
- Encourage you to apply the Word of God to everyday life
- Help you to share your faith with others
- They are straightforward, practical, non-controversial and inexpensive.

WEC INTERNATIONAL is involved in gospel outreach, church planting and discipleship training using every possible means including radio, literature, medical work, rural development schemes, correspondence courses and telephone counselling. Nearly 2,000 workers are involved in their fields and sending bases.

Find out more from the following website:

www.wec-int.org.uk

A full list of over fifty 'Geared for Growth' studies can be obtained from:

www.gearedforgrowth.co.uk

orders@gearedforgrowth.co.uk

info@gearedforgrowth.co.uk

wordworldwideinternational@gmail.com